IS-909: Community Preparedness: Implementing Simple Activities for Everyone

By

Fema

10/31/2013

IS-909 - Community Preparedness: Implementing Simple Activities for Everyone

Welcome

Community members are the key to our Nation's preparedness and resilience. As such, we need to:

- Support the development of prepared, vigilant, and engaged communities.
- Foster strategic partnerships among:
  - The private sector.
  - Nongovernmental organizations.
  - Foundations.
  - Community-based organizations.

The purpose of this course is to present a model program for community preparedness.

Course Objectives

After this course, you should be able to:

- Identify the definition of preparedness.
- Describe the role of individuals and households in preparedness.
- Identify community preparedness principles.
- Describe the purpose of community-based preparedness activities.
- Identify the steps for planning and conducting a community-based preparedness program.
- Identify resources for supporting community-based preparedness programs.

Preparedness: Definition

Preparedness is defined as actions taken to plan, organize, equip, train, and exercise to build and sustain the capabilities necessary to:

- Prevent,
- Protect against,
- Mitigate the effects of,

* Respond to, and
* Recover from those threats that pose the greatest risk.

Presidential Policy Directive/PPD-8: National Preparedness

* Introduction
* National Preparedness Goal
* National Preparedness System
* Building and Sustaining Preparedness
* National Preparedness Report
* Roles and Responsibilities
* Definitions

March 30, 2011
PRESIDENTIAL POLICY DIRECTIVE/PPD-8
SUBJECT: National Preparedness

This directive is aimed at strengthening the security and resilience of the United States through systematic preparation for the threats that pose the greatest risk to the security of the Nation, including acts of terrorism, cyber attacks, pandemics, and catastrophic natural disasters. Our national preparedness is the shared responsibility of all levels of government, the private and nonprofit sectors, and individual citizens. Everyone can contribute to safeguarding the Nation from harm. As such, while this directive is intended to galvanize action by the Federal Government, it is also aimed at facilitating an integrated, all-of-Nation, capabilities-based approach to preparedness.

Therefore, I hereby direct the development of a national preparedness goal that identifies the core capabilities necessary for preparedness and a national preparedness system to guide activities that will enable the Nation to achieve the goal. The system will allow the Nation to track the progress of our ability to build and improve the capabilities necessary to prevent, protect against, mitigate the effects of, respond to, and recover from those threats that pose the greatest risk to the security of the Nation.

The Assistant to the President for Homeland Security and Counterterrorism shall coordinate the interagency development of an implementation plan for completing the national preparedness goal and national preparedness system. The implementation plan shall be submitted to me within 60 days from the date of this directive, and shall assign departmental responsibilities and delivery timelines for the development of the national planning frameworks and associated interagency operational plans described below.

National Preparedness Goal

Within 180 days from the date of this directive, the Secretary of Homeland Security shall develop and submit the national preparedness goal to me, through the Assistant to the President for Homeland Security and Counterterrorism. The Secretary shall coordinate this effort with other executive departments and agencies, and consult with State, local, tribal, and territorial governments, the private and nonprofit sectors, and the public.

The national preparedness goal shall be informed by the risk of specific threats and vulnerabilities – taking into account regional variations - and include concrete, measurable, and prioritized objectives to mitigate that risk. The national preparedness goal shall define the core capabilities necessary to prepare for the specific types of incidents that pose the greatest risk to the security of the Nation, and shall emphasize actions aimed at achieving an integrated, layered, and all-of-Nation preparedness approach that optimizes the use of available resources. The national preparedness goal shall reflect the policy direction outlined in the National Security Strategy (May 2010), applicable Presidential Policy Directives, Homeland Security Presidential Directives, National Security Presidential Directives, and national strategies, as well as guidance from the Interagency Policy Committee process. The goal shall be reviewed regularly to evaluate consistency with these policies, evolving conditions, and the National Incident Management System.

National Preparedness System

The national preparedness system shall be an integrated set of guidance, programs, and processes that will enable the Nation to meet the national preparedness goal. Within 240 days from the date of this directive, the Secretary of Homeland Security shall develop and submit a description of the national preparedness system to me, through the Assistant to the President for Homeland Security and Counterterrorism. The Secretary shall coordinate this effort with other executive departments and agencies, and consult with State, local, tribal, and territorial governments, the private and nonprofit sectors, and the public.

The national preparedness system shall be designed to help guide the domestic efforts of all levels of government, the private and nonprofit sectors, and the public to build and sustain the capabilities outlined in the national preparedness goal. The national preparedness system shall include guidance for planning, organization, equipment, training, and exercises to build and maintain domestic capabilities. It shall provide an all-of-Nation approach for building and sustaining a cycle of preparedness activities over time.

The national preparedness system shall include a series of integrated national planning frameworks, covering prevention, protection, mitigation, response, and recovery. The frameworks shall be built upon scalable, flexible, and adaptable coordinating structures to align key roles and responsibilities to deliver the necessary capabilities. The frameworks shall be coordinated under a unified system with a common terminology and approach, built around basic plans that support the all-hazards approach to preparedness and functional or incident annexes to describe any unique requirements for particular threats or scenarios, as needed. Each framework shall describe how actions taken in the framework are coordinated with relevant actions described in the other frameworks across the preparedness spectrum.

The national preparedness system shall include an interagency operational plan to support each national planning framework. Each interagency operational plan shall include a more detailed concept of operations; description of critical tasks and responsibilities; detailed resource, personnel, and sourcing requirements; and specific provisions for the rapid integration of resources and personnel.

All executive departments and agencies with roles in the national planning frameworks shall develop department-level operational plans to support the interagency operational plans, as needed. Each national planning framework shall include guidance to support corresponding planning for State, local, tribal, and territorial governments.

The national preparedness system shall include resource guidance, such as arrangements enabling the ability to share personnel. It shall provide equipment guidance aimed at nationwide interoperability; and shall provide guidance for national training and exercise programs, to facilitate our ability to build and sustain the capabilities defined in the national preparedness goal and evaluate progress toward meeting the goal.

The national preparedness system shall include recommendations and guidance to support preparedness planning for businesses, communities, families, and individuals.

The national preparedness system shall include a comprehensive approach to assess national preparedness that uses consistent methodology to measure the operational readiness of national capabilities at the time of assessment, with clear, objective, and quantifiable performance measures, against the target capability levels identified in the national preparedness goal.

Building and Sustaining Preparedness

The Secretary of Homeland Security shall coordinate a comprehensive campaign to build and sustain national preparedness, including public outreach and community-based and private-sector programs to enhance national resilience, the provision of Federal financial assistance, preparedness efforts by the Federal Government, and national research and development efforts.

National Preparedness Report

Within 1 year from the date of this directive, the Secretary of Homeland Security shall submit the first national preparedness report based on the national preparedness goal to me, through the Assistant to the President for Homeland Security and Counterterrorism. The Secretary shall coordinate this effort with other executive departments and agencies and consult with State, local, tribal, and territorial governments, the private and nonprofit sectors, and the public. The Secretary shall submit the report annually in sufficient time to allow it to inform the preparation of my Administration's budget.

Roles and Responsibilities

The Assistant to the President for Homeland Security and Counterterrorism shall periodically review progress toward achieving the national preparedness goal.

The Secretary of Homeland Security is responsible for coordinating the domestic all-hazards preparedness efforts of all executive departments and agencies, in consultation with State, local, tribal, and territorial governments, nongovernmental organizations, private-sector partners, and the general public; and for developing the national preparedness goal.

The heads of all executive departments and agencies with roles in prevention, protection, mitigation, response, and recovery are responsible for national preparedness efforts, including department-specific operational plans, as needed, consistent with their statutory roles and responsibilities.

Nothing in this directive is intended to alter or impede the ability to carry out the authorities of executive departments and agencies to perform their responsibilities under law and consistent with applicable legal authorities and other Presidential guidance. This directive shall be implemented consistent with relevant authorities, including the Post-Katrina Emergency Management Reform Act of 2006 and its assignment of responsibilities with respect to the Administrator of the Federal Emergency Management Agency.

Nothing in this directive is intended to interfere with the authority of the Attorney General or Director of the Federal Bureau of Investigation with regard to the direction, conduct, control, planning, organization, equipment, training, exercises, or other activities concerning domestic counterterrorism, intelligence, and law enforcement activities.

Nothing in this directive shall limit the authority of the Secretary of Defense with regard to the command and control, planning, organization, equipment, training, exercises, employment, or other activities of Department of Defense forces, or the allocation of Department of Defense resources.

If resolution on a particular matter called for in this directive cannot be reached between or among executive departments and agencies, the matter shall be referred to me through the Assistant to the President for Homeland Security and Counterterrorism.

This directive replaces Homeland Security Presidential Directive (HSPD)-8 (National Preparedness), issued December 17, 2003, and HSPD-8 Annex I (National Planning), issued December 4, 2007, which are hereby rescinded, except for paragraph 44 of HSPD-8 Annex I. Individual plans developed under HSPD-8 and Annex I remain in effect until rescinded or otherwise replaced.

Definitions

For the purposes of this directive:

(a) The term "national preparedness" refers to the actions taken to plan, organize, equip, train, and exercise to build and sustain the capabilities necessary to prevent, protect against, mitigate the effects of, respond to, and recover from those threats that pose the greatest risk to the security of the Nation.

(b) The term "security" refers to the protection of the Nation and its people, vital interests, and way of life.

(c) The term "resilience" refers to the ability to adapt to changing conditions and withstand and rapidly recover from disruption due to emergencies.

(d) The term "prevention" refers to those capabilities necessary to avoid, prevent, or stop a threatened or actual act of terrorism. Prevention capabilities include, but are not limited to, information sharing and warning; domestic counterterrorism; and preventing the acquisition or use of weapons of mass destruction (WMD). For purposes of the prevention framework called for in this directive, the term "prevention" refers to preventing imminent threats.

(e) The term "protection" refers to those capabilities necessary to secure the homeland against acts of terrorism and manmade or natural disasters. Protection capabilities include, but are not limited to, defense against WMD threats; defense of agriculture and food; critical infrastructure protection; protection of key leadership and events; border security; maritime security; transportation security; immigration security; and cybersecurity.

(f) The term "mitigation" refers to those capabilities necessary to reduce loss of life and property by lessening the impact of disasters. Mitigation capabilities include, but are not limited to, community-wide risk reduction projects; efforts to improve the resilience of critical infrastructure and key resource lifelines; risk reduction for specific vulnerabilities from natural hazards or acts of terrorism; and initiatives to reduce future risks after a disaster has occurred.

(g) The term "response" refers to those capabilities necessary to save lives, protect property and the environment, and meet basic human needs after an incident has occurred.

(h) The term "recovery" refers to those capabilities necessary to assist communities affected by an incident to recover effectively, including, but not limited to, rebuilding infrastructure systems; providing adequate interim and long-term housing for survivors; restoring health, social, and community services; promoting economic development; and restoring natural and cultural resources.

Preparedness: A Shared Responsibility

Preparedness is the shared responsibility of all levels of government, the private and nonprofit sectors, and individual citizens.

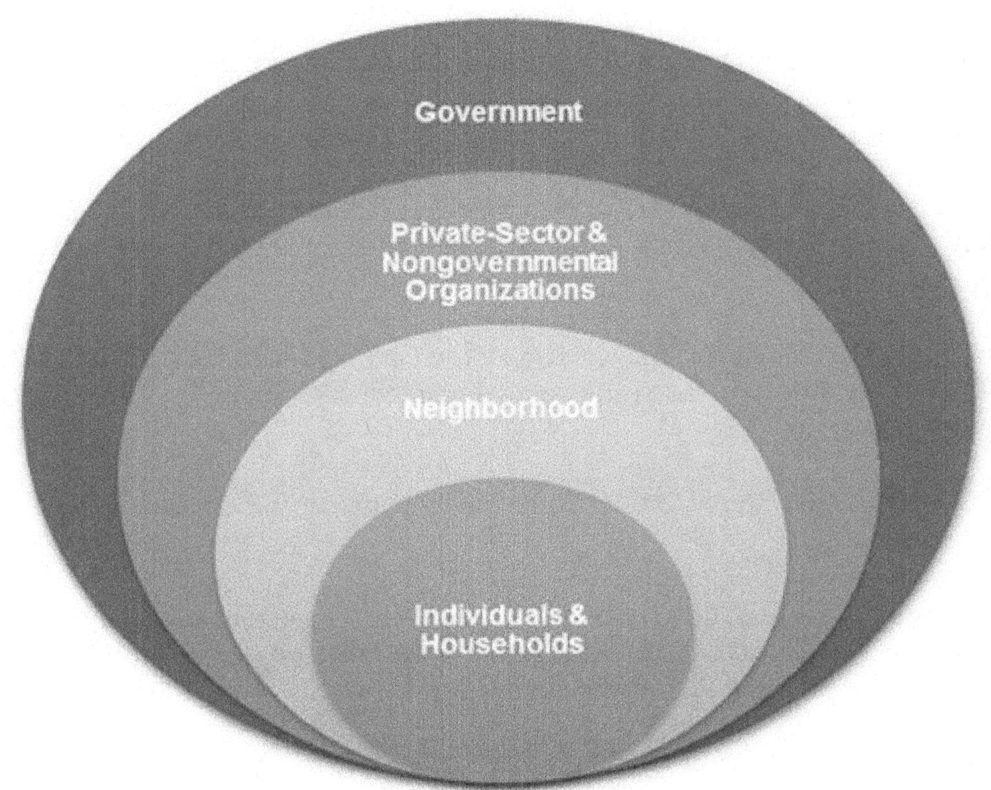

Individual and Households

Individuals and households are at the core of our Nation's preparedness. A community's ability to respond to or recover from a disaster depends on the level of preparedness of every member.

However, a 2009 Citizen Corps national survey found that 29 percent of Americans have not prepared because they think that emergency responders will help them, and that over 60 percent expect to rely on emergency responders in the first 72 hours following a disaster.

The reality is that in a disaster, first responders and emergency workers may not be able to reach everyone right away. In addition, providers may not be able to restore critical services, such as power, immediately.

Community Preparedness Best Practices

NARRATOR: This presentation tells the story of how Mayor Melvin "Kip" Holden succeeded in engaging the City of Baton Rouge, in East Baton Rouge Parish, to be better prepared.

JOANNE H. MOREAU (Director of Homeland Security and Emergency Preparedness): It's really, really important to have the community engaged in the process, because government can't do everything for everyone.

NARRATOR: While responding to disasters, Mayor Holden and his staff began to realize that many of the issues they faced repeatedly could be eliminated if the public was better prepared.

RANNAH GRAY: Our current mayor, Kip Holden, worked with his staff at the Mayor's Office of Homeland Security and Emergency Preparedness with an idea that we need more public education.

NARRATOR: The first step was to ask others how outreach and education could be improved.

JOANNE H. MOREAU: While our message was kind of sporadic and always public safety, we weren't quite sure if we were doing the best that we could. So that was the basis for our survey, to find out: where do we go from here?

RANNAH GRAY: And one of the things that really came to light was there's such a need, so many people didn't know what to do, didn't have a plan, separated from families, didn't know how to get in contact, separated from prescription medicines.

NARRATOR: Based on survey results, the Mayor's Office developed an outreach campaign for the whole community known as Red Stick Ready.

RANNAH GRAY: We like to say that our audience is everyone. And we have lots of messages and we try to target. If we're talking about a senior population, we go work with our Council of Aging on any programs that might target seniors. If we're talking to children, we try to get into the schools.

JOANNE H. MOREAU: Working with the children, and with such an emphasis on the children, we wanted a tool that could reach them.

MAYOR HOLDEN: We have what they call Mayor Mouse, and Mayor Mouse basically is operated to go to various schools. In a span of, I think, 2 months, we took in roughly about almost 3,000 kids at various sites to talk to them about different safety things.

JOANNE H. MOREAU: So Mayor Mouse, our Mayor, along with the real mayor actually goes to that event and interacts with the people that are present. You'll be quite surprised at how the elected official mouse makes all the difference with the children.

JOANNE H. MOREAU: The children are selected by the teacher and come in and for several hours, run the city and the fire chief works with the child that is the fire chief. So there's a lot about interaction, they learn about their position prior to an event, they have to do public speaking because there's a series of briefings that are held and the kids have to stand up and talk about what they're doing as the fire chief.

MAYOR HOLDEN: We'll often talk to young kids and say to them that you need to plan an evacuation route. We talk to parents and say you need to plan an evacuation route. And then we feature the fire chief and we feature hazmat and other components of the fire department to talk about fire safety.

RANNAH GRAY: It's so important for local officials to communicate directly with their community and with the public. There's no better spokespersons that they want to see and hear from than their local elected officials, and this can be just highly effective in carrying this message out to the community.

RANNAH GRAY: We feel that we've really made strides in teaching the public.

JOANNE H. MOREAU: Where we see Red Stick Ready going is that other communities, and we do share with a lot of communities, that we have a common message about preparedness.

RANNAH GRAY: We won't be satisfied until everyone that we talk to is ready for an emergency.

JOANNE H. MOREAU: It's community preparedness, and it's a community, one household at a time.

Community Preparedness Principles

Citizen Corps, an organization created to help coordinate volunteer activities, established the following community preparedness principles:

- **Collaboration:** Government must collaborate with community leaders from all sectors for effective planning and capacity building.
- **Integration:** Nongovernmental assets and resources must be fully integrated into government plans, preparations, and disaster response.
- **Personal/Organizational Preparedness:** Everyone in America should be fully aware, trained, and practiced on how to prevent, protect, mitigate, prepare for, and respond to all threats and hazards.

- **Volunteer Service:** Citizen activism and volunteer service provide ongoing support for community safety and critical surge capacity in response and recovery.

Community-Based Activities

This course introduces you to a program for promoting personal and community preparedness through engaging activities for individuals, neighbors, or households.

These activities are a set of building blocks. You can:

- Mix and match the activities based on the needs of your target audience or time available. Most activities can be completed during a 15-minute to 60-minute session.
- Adapt the materials to include critical local information, such as information on local hazards, local alerts and warnings, and local community response resources and protocols.

Remember, preparedness does not have to be complex or overly time consuming. Rather, it should motivate, empower, and engage the whole community.

Program Materials

The program materials include Program Leader and Facilitator Guides and Handout Masters. Click on a document cover to access a copy.

This course includes the contents of the Program Leader Guide. Click this link to access Spanish-language versions of these documents.

Facilitator Guide

Within the Facilitator Guide, the first pages of each preparedness topic provide the facilitator with the overall purpose of the session, suggested preparation steps and materials, and presentation tips.

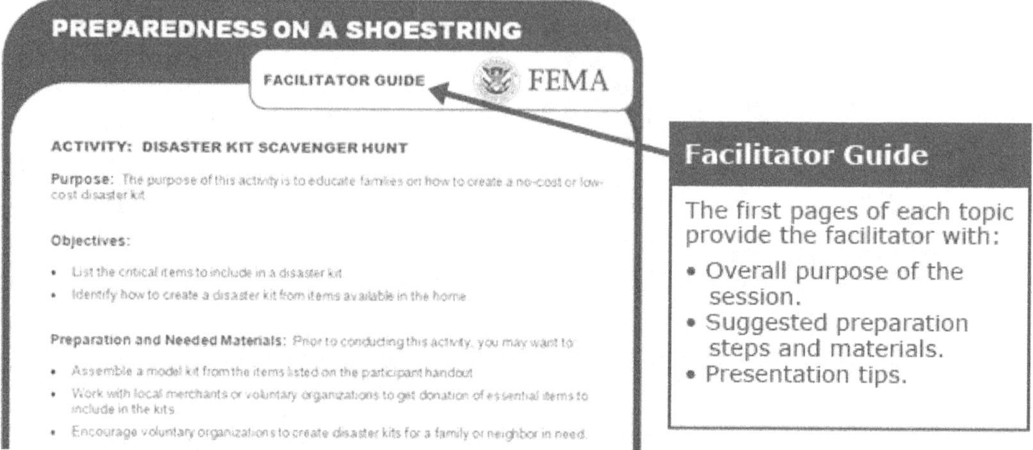

Handouts

Accompanying the Facilitator Guide are handouts for the participants to use during the session or as "take away" materials.

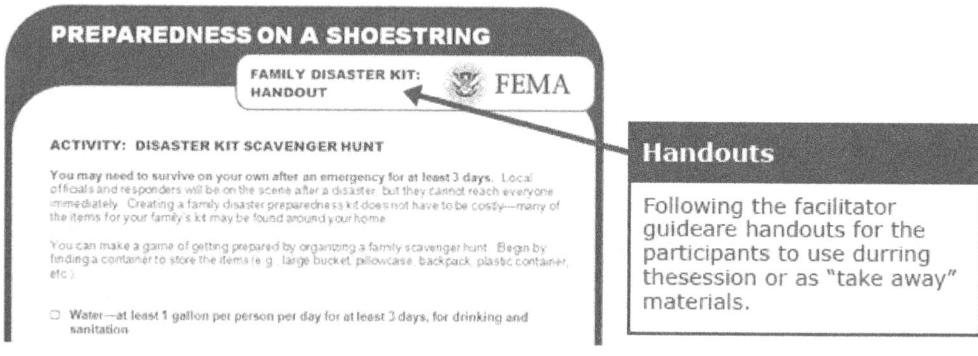

The Preparedness Topics

Below is a list of preparedness activities included in this program:

Core Preparedness Topics

Title	Information and Activities on . . .	Approx. Length
Preparedness on a Shoestring	Creating a no-cost or low-cost disaster kit	30 – 60 minutes
Where Is Everybody?	Developing a communications plan	20 minutes
Who Can You Count On? Who Counts on You?	Establishing a personal support network	20 minutes
Easy Out: Getting to Safety	Planning for and practicing an evacuation	30 minutes
Storm Safe — Sheltering in Place	Staying safe when evacuation is not an option	20 – 40 minutes
Disaster Plan Dress Rehearsal	Practicing your disaster plan	30 – 60 minutes

Hazard-Reduction Topics

Title	Information and Activities on . . .	Approx. Length
Hunting Home Hazards	Identifying and reducing home hazards	30 – 60 minutes
An Ounce of Fire Prevention	Identifying and reducing fire risks	30 minutes
Putting Out Fires	Using a fire extinguisher	30 – 60 minutes
Home Safe Home	Implementing simple risk-reduction (mitigation) measures	30 – 60 minutes
Safeguarding Your Valuables	Protecting important items and documents	30 minutes

Specialized Preparedness Topics

Title	Information and Activities on . . .	Approx. Length
Pet/Service Animal Preparedness	Taking care of pets and service animals during a disaster	30 minutes
Rx for Readiness	Starting a "Stay Healthy" Kit and plan	30 minutes
Going Off Grid: Utility Outages	Preparing for utility outages	20 – 40 minutes

| Coming Home After a Disaster | Planning for recovery from disaster | 20 minutes |
| Preparedness: The Whole Community | Understanding emergency management and response roles and getting involved | 30 – 90 minutes |

You can mix and match the topics based on the needs of your audience. In addition, you may adjust the times by modifying the activities demonstrated during the session.

Planning Your Program

To plan your preparedness program, you may want to complete the following steps:

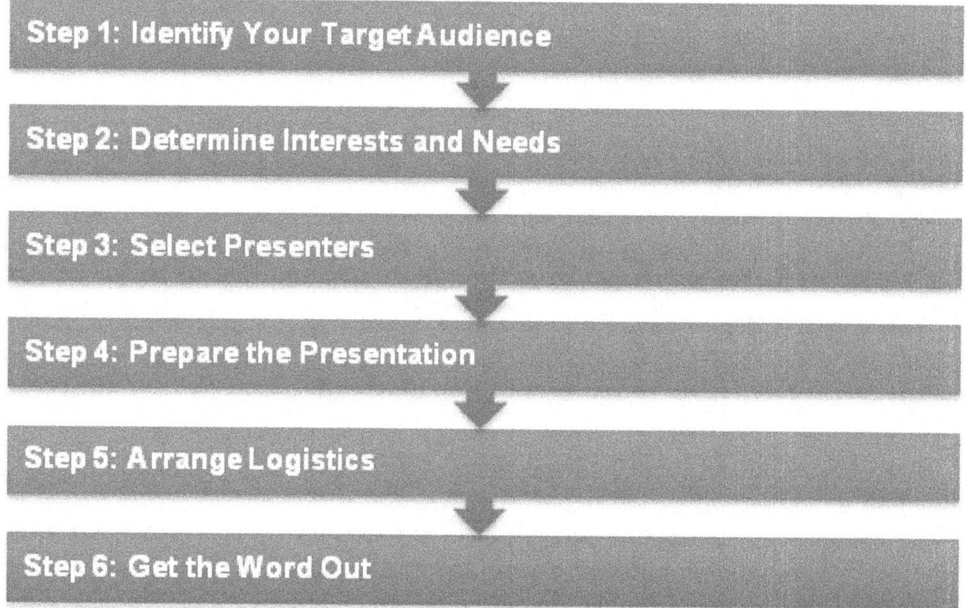

Step 1: Identify Your Target Audience

To identify your target audience:

- Think about who would benefit from this program.
- Ask for input from community leaders and organizations.
- Make sure to be inclusive of all members of the community.

Step 2: Determine Interests and Needs

Now that you have identified the members of your target audience, ask yourself:

- What will motivate these individuals to attend preparedness session(s)?
- What do you think participants will hope to gain or learn?
- Which topics are of most interest to them?
- How much time will individuals want to spend at a session?
- How likely are they to return if you offered multiple sessions?
- What day, time, and location will be best?
- What is the ideal mix of people to help foster networking and sustainability after the session?
- Will everyone be able to access the training location and be comfortable in the room?
- Will everyone be able to hear you, use the handouts, and complete the activities?

Use the answers to these questions to select the topics to be included in your program and determine how to schedule your session(s).

Step 3: Select Presenters

A facilitator with effective communications skills should be able to conduct most of the sessions. However, it is recommended that individuals with the following expertise present the two sessions below.

Title	Recommended Presenter
Putting Out Fires	Fire service personnel
Preparedness: The Whole Community	Emergency management personnel

Local nongovernmental groups, such as the American Red Cross or Community Emergency Response Team (CERT) members, are invaluable resources to help with presentations or prepare you to conduct the sessions.

Suggested Presenters

Title	Recommended Presenter
Putting Out Fires	Fire service personnel
Preparedness: The Whole Community	Emergency management personnel

Title	Optional Individuals To Involve
Preparedness on a Shoestring	Emergency management personnel
Where Is Everybody?	Emergency management personnel
Who Can You Count On? Who Counts on You?	Representatives from functional needs community
Easy Out: Getting to Safety	Emergency management personnel
Storm Safe — Sheltering in Place	Emergency management personnel
Disaster Plan Dress Rehearsal	Emergency management personnel
Hunting Home Hazards	Fire service personnel
An Ounce of Fire Prevention	Fire service personnel
Home Safe Home	Construction expert or structural engineer/mitigation specialist
Pet/Service Animal Preparedness	Local animal shelter personnel/veterinarian
Rx for Readiness	Local medical or public health personnel
Going Off Grid: Utility Outages	Local public works personnel/utility company representative
Coming Home After a Disaster	Construction expert or structural engineer/emergency management personnel

Step 4: Prepare the Presentation

The facilitator's preparation and conduct of the session are keys to the effectiveness of this program.

Presenters should:

- Read the materials thoroughly.
- Complete all activities and be prepared to answer the questions that the participants will likely ask while completing the activities.
- Draft your own notes in the margins of the materials.
- Add personal experiences to help explain the important points.
- Tailor the material with information on local hazards, local alerts and warnings, and local community response resources and protocols. Also, you may want to emphasize different information (e.g., apartment evacuation vs. single homes) to meet your audience's needs.
- Rehearse with a small group and ask for suggestions for enhancing the delivery.

Facilitation Tips

- **Make yourself part of the group.** Do not separate yourself physically from the group by standing behind a podium or a table. Feel free to move around the room while you are speaking.
- **Do not read or lecture to the group.** Think back to the last class that you attended. If the instructor lectured incessantly, chances are that you tuned out and did not learn much. This package is a guide, not your script. Flexibility is the key to success. You may modify discussion questions to meet the needs of the group. If you do not like or do not understand a question, change it.
- **Don't answer questions if you are not sure of the answers.** If a participant asks you a question to which you do not know the answer:
  - Tell the participant that you do not know the answer.
  - Explain that you will find the answer and get back to the participant.
- **Check for understanding.** Sticking to the agenda is important, but do not move to the next activity before ensuring that the group understands what has already been discussed. You can check understanding by asking for volunteers to summarize concepts and fill in gaps during your transitions.
- **Watch for both verbal and nonverbal responses and clues.** Use your observations to keep the session running smoothly.

Step 5: Arrange Logistics

It is important to arrange logistics, including:

- Notifications.
- Room setups.
- Safety.
- Supplies, materials, and refreshments.

Forming partnerships with other organizations or getting sponsorship from the business community can help defray some of the expenses for supplies, materials, and refreshments.

Faith-based organizations, libraries, civic associations, schools, or government office buildings may have space for hosting the sessions.

Logistics Checklist Use the checklist below to organize and take care of all logistics.

Notifications

- Have all participants and presenters been notified of the time and location? ☐ Yes ☐ No

- Has any needed transportation been arranged? ☐ Yes ☐ No

Condition of Room

- Is the training room clean? ☐ Yes ☐ No

- Does the room accommodate individuals with disabilities? ☐ Yes ☐ No

- Is seating capacity adequate? ☐ Yes ☐ No

- Is seating arrangement (round tables, conference tables) satisfactory? ☐ Yes ☐ No

Safety

- Are there adequate exits from the room? ☐ Yes ☐ No

- Are exits clearly marked? ☐ Yes ☐ No

- Do any hazards exist (e.g., loose wires/cables, narrow aisles, loose carpet, sharp edges on tables, etc.)? ☐ Yes ☐ No

Supplies, Materials, and Refreshments

- Do you have all needed supporting materials? ☐ Yes ☐ No

- Are there sufficient copies of all handout materials? ☐ Yes ☐ No

- Are there pens and paper for the participants to take notes? ☐ Yes ☐ No

- Are there badges or name tents for the participants? ☐ Yes ☐ No

- Do you have feedback questionnaires for the participants? ☐ Yes ☐ No

- Do you plan to serve refreshments? ☐ Yes ☐ No

Step 6: Get the Word Out

You may need to let your target audience know about the preparedness program. Below are suggestions for getting the word out:

- Telephone calls to neighborhood associations and faith-based organizations
- Email messages to community members
- Newsletter articles
- Web, social media, or blog postings
- Public service announcements
- Local cable television notices

Forming a partnership with local media outlets can be invaluable for promoting your program and recognizing contributions from presenters and others.

Taking photographs of preparedness sessions may be useful for promoting future sessions. Remember, you should get releases from individuals before publishing the photographs.

Getting Feedback

At the end of your session, you may want to get feedback from your participants. Below are sample questions that you can ask:

Sample Feedback Questions
<ul><li>What was the most effective portion of the presentation?</li><li>How could we improve this presentation?</li><li>Following this presentation, what preparedness actions do you plan to take?</li><li>What additional preparedness information would be helpful?</li></ul>

Acknowledging Accomplishments

Following your session, you may want to take the following actions:

- **Thank-You Notes:** Make sure to send thank-you notes to individuals and organizations who helped with presentations or provided sponsorship.
- **Follow-Up:** Contact participants to see if they are implementing preparedness actions.
- **Certificates:** Present certificates to participants who complete the entire program.
- **Articles or Postings:** Feature preparedness accomplishments in articles or Web postings to reinforce actions and encourage others.

Program Materials

Click on a link below to access the program materials:

English Versions

- Program Leader Guide
- Facilitator Guide
- Handout Masters

Spanish Versions

- Program Leader Guide
- Facilitator Guide
- Handout Masters

Additional Resources

Below are additional resources that you may want to use in planning and conducting your preparedness program.

- **Citizen Preparedness Publications**
  - Preparing for Disaster – FEMA 475
  - Helping Children Cope With Disaster – FEMA 478
  - Food and Water in an Emergency – FEMA 477
  - Emergency Financial First Aid Kit – FEMA 532

    Web Site: www.citizencorps.gov/ready/cc_pubs.shtm

- **Ready.gov**
  - Ready Family Emergency Plans
  - Hazard-Specific Information
  - Family Communications Plan and Wallet Card

- o   Printer-Friendly Supplies

    Web Site: www.ready.gov

- **FEMA.gov**
  - o   FEMA Office of Disability Integration and Coordination

    Web Site: www.fema.gov/office-disability-integration-and-coordination

- **Red Cross**
  - o   Ready Quick-Reference
  - o   Disaster Preparedness for People With Disabilities

    Web Site: www.redcross.org

- **Weather Information**
  - o   Weather Information
    Web Site: www.weather.gov
  - o   NOAA Weather Radio All Hazards
    Web Site: www.nws.noaa.gov/nwr/

- **Flu.gov**
  Web Site: www.flu.gov

- **Foodsafety.gov**
  Web Site: www.foodsafety.gov

Course Summary

Congratulations! You should now be ready to implement an activity-based community preparedness program.

Every day across our Nation, neighbors help neighbors to cope with emergencies. These simple acts of kindness are what made this country great. Helping individuals to be better prepared will make us a more resilient country.

www.ingramcontent.com/pod-product-compliance
Lightning Source LLC
Chambersburg PA
CBHW081854250726
48659CB00008B/2758